D0569580

WW kitchen collection

Flavours

Harissa chicken skewers, p38

Tofu & mushroom stir-fry, page 102

Paprika fish & fennel stew, page 30

Piri piri pork, page 84

WW kitchen collection

Flavours

EGGS We use medium eggs, unless otherwise stated. Pregnant women, the elderly and children should avoid recipes with eggs which are raw or not fully cooked if not produced under the British Lion code of practice.

FRUIT AND VEGETABLES Recipes use medium-size fruit and veg, unless otherwise stated.

LIGHT SOFT CHEESE Where a recipe uses reduced-fat soft cheese, we mean a soft cheese with 30% less fat than its full-fat equivalent.

LOW-FAT SPREAD When a recipe uses a low-fat spread, we mean a spread with a fat content of no more than 39%.

MICROWAVES If we have used a microwave in any of our recipes, the timings will be for an 850-watt microwave oven.

PREP AND COOK TIMES These are approximate and meant to be guidelines only. Prep time includes all steps up to and following the main cooking time(s). Stated cook times may vary according to your oven.

VEGETARIAN ITALIAN-STYLE HARD CHEESE Where we reference this in vegetarian recipes, we mean a cheese similar to Parmesan (which is not vegetarian) but which is suitable for vegetarians.

GLUTEN FREE Recipes displaying the gluten free icon include ingredients that naturally do not contain gluten, but may also contain processed products, such as sauces, stock cubes and spice mixes. If so, you should ensure that those products do not include any gluten-containing ingredients (wheat, barley or rye) — these will be highlighted in the ingredients list on the product's label. Manufacturers may also indicate whether there is a chance that their product may have been accidentally contaminated with gluten during the manufacturing process. For more information and guidance on gluten-free products, visit www.coeliac.org.uk

SMARTPOINTS® have been calculated using the values for generic foods, not brands (except where stated). Tracking using branded items may affect the recorded SmartPoints.

WEIGHT WATCHERS PUBLICATIONS TEAM
Samantha Rees, Nicola Hill, Ruby Bamford, Kim Clayden

FOR SEVEN PUBLISHING LTD
FOOD
Food editor Nadine Brown
Associate food editor Ella Tarn
Nutritionist Alexandra Harris

EDITORIAL
Editor-in-Chief Helen Renshaw
Editor Ward Hellewell
Sub-editor Christine Faughlin

DESIGN & PHOTOGRAPHY
Art director Liz Baird
Photography Kris Kirkham
Food stylist Sarah Cook
Assisted by Anna Horne
Prop stylist Tonia Shuttleworth

ACCOUNT MANAGEMENT
Account manager Gina Cavaciuti
Group publishing director Kirsten Price

PRODUCTION
Production director Sophie Dillon
Colour reproduction by F1 Colour
Printed in the UK by CPI Colour

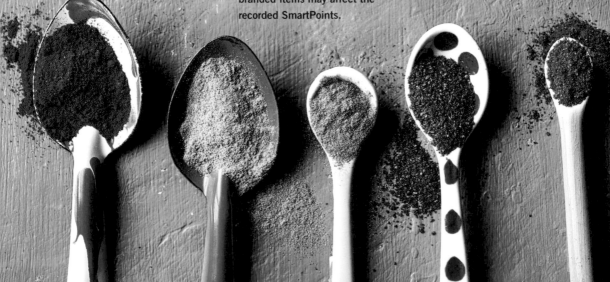

Contents

Seven C3

Produced by Seven Publishing on behalf of Weight Watchers International, Inc. Published July 2018. All rights reserved. No part of this publication may be reproduced, stored in a retrieval system or transmitted in any form by any means, electronic, mechanical photocopying, recording or otherwise, without the prior written permission of Seven Publishing. First published in Great Britain by Seven Publishing Ltd.

Seven Publishing Ltd, 3-7 Herbal Hill, London EC1R 5EJ www.seven.co.uk

This book is copyright under the Berne Convention. No reproduction without permission. All rights reserved.

10 9 8 7 6 5 4 3 2 1

© 2018 Weight Watchers International, Inc. All rights reserved. The SmartPoints Weight-Loss System and these materials are proprietary to Weight Watchers International, Inc. and are licensed to Weight Watchers members solely for their personal use in losing and controlling their weight. Any other use, including but not limited to reproduction or distribution in any form or medium, is strictly prohibited. NOT FOR RESALE. WEIGHT WATCHERS, POINTS and SmartPoints are the registered trademarks of Weight Watchers International, Inc.

A CIP catalogue record for this book is available from the British Library. ISBN: 978-1-9996673-0-6

WHEN YOU SEE THESE SYMBOLS:

0 SmartPoints value — Tells you how many SmartPoints are in the recipe.

✳ Indicates a recipe is suitable for freezing.

GF Indicates a recipe is gluten free (see page 6).

V Indicates a recipe is vegetarian.

Get ready to explore a world of taste with this collection of 46 flavour-packed recipes from the Weight Watchers kitchen. You'll find everything from **spicy** Indian curries and Tex-Mex chilli to fragrant dishes from the Middle-East, slow-cooked casseroles and **fresh, zingy** Asian stir-fries. Most of the recipes are based around our zero Points foods®, with fresh herbs, spices, marinades and other **flavour-boosting** ingredients to help you transform the simplest of dishes into something **really special**. These aren't just recipes for 'foodies' – they're meals you can make every day to keep things fresh and **exciting** at the dinner table. Every recipe has been tried and tested by the WW Kitchen team and we've included the SmartPoints for them all, making it **easier** to relax and enjoy cooking and eating healthy, tasty food.

9 FLAVOUR-PACKED INGREDIENTS

Want to get a bit more adventurous with flavours? Add these to your storecupboard.

MISO
Made from fermented soya beans, miso has a rich, savoury flavour and is popular in Japanese cooking. It comes as a paste that can be added to soup, sauces, marinades and salad dressings. Use it to add flavour to blander foods, such as tofu or aubergines. **Try: Miso roast chicken, p42.**

HARISSA
A fragrant paste made with chillies and other spices, harissa is common in North African cuisine. Use it as a rub for meat before cooking, or add it to sauces, dressings and soups to spice them up. **Try: Harissa pork with cumin-spiced 'noodles', p64.**

WASABI
The green paste most often associated with sushi is made from the root of a plant from the cabbage family. It has a mustardy flavour like horseradish and is a good addition to grilled meats, or used to spice up mayonnaise. As well as the paste, it's available in powdered form. **Try: Salmon teriyaki burger with wasabi mayonnaise, p18.**

OYSTER SAUCE
Although it is actually made from oysters, don't let that put you off if you're not a fan. Oyster sauce has a rich, savoury flavour with a hint of sweetness that makes it great for stir-fries or for using as a glaze for chicken or fish. **Try: Salmon fillets with a ginger & lemongrass crust, p28.**

CHORIZO
A cured pork sausage that's flavoured with smoked paprika, chorizo has an intense flavour so you can use it in small amounts to add interest to other dishes. Chop and add it to soups and paella or other rice dishes, or use thin slices as a pizza topping. **Try: Chilli prawns & chorizo rice bowl, p26.**

CHIPOTLE
Chipotles are smoked chillies which can be bought as a powder, dried flakes or as a paste. A lot of Mexican recipes use chipotle for its smoky, spicy flavour – it's great in casseroles and goes well with chicken, as well as pulses. **Try: Chicken & chipotle stew with quinoa, p40.**

POMEGRANATE MOLASSES
This Middle-Eastern ingredient is pomegranate juice that's been reduced to a thick syrup. It's fruity and tangy – think of it like a sweeter balsamic vinegar and use it in the same way, in dressings, sauces marinades or brushed on roasted meats or vegetables. **Try: Turkish-style stuffed aubergines, p90.**

WORCESTERSHIRE SAUCE
A classic British ingredient made from a secret recipe that's thought to include anchovies, cloves and tamarind. It's great for bringing out the flavour of meat, so add a dash to chilli con carne, beef stir-fries or meatloaf. **Try: Sticky bourbon pork, p80.**

SESAME OIL
With its nutty, toasty flavour, sesame oil is a mainstay of Asian cooking. You only need a small amount and it's usually used as a flavouring, rather than a cooking oil. Add a dash to stir-fries or use it in dressings for Asian-style salads. **Try: Spiced nasi goreng, p88.**

EASY WAYS TO BOOST FLAVOUR

Discover how to create tasty dishes every time with these top tips...

TOAST YOUR SPICES

Spices, seeds and nuts all benefit from a light toasting before you use them. Whole spices, like coriander or cumin seeds, as well as ground spices can be toasted. Do it in a dry frying pan over a medium heat, shaking the pan continuously so they don't burn. Tip them onto a plate as soon as they start to release their aroma.

FRESH HERBS

Fresh herbs like parsley, coriander, basil and dill add loads of flavour to any dish. Roughly chop or tear them first, and add them at the end of cooking to preserve their flavour.

BROWN MEAT

Sear meat in a very hot pan misted with calorie controlled cooking spray until it's browned all over before using it in a casserole or stew. It will give the finished dish a deeper, richer flavour and more appealing colour.

COOK IN STOCK

When cooking rice, couscous, bulgur wheat or other grains, try using chicken or vegetable stock made from stock cubes instead of just water.

ROASTING VEGETABLES

Bring out the natural flavours of vegetables by roasting them. Spread them on a baking sheet, mist with calorie controlled cooking spray then roast in a hot oven until caramelised and tender.

SPICE RUBS

Dry spice rubs are a great way to add flavour without the extra oil that is in many marinades. Buy them ready-made or make your own by blending your favourite spiced and dried herbs. Rub the mix all over the meat, and set aside so the flavours can develop, before grilling, pan-frying or roasting.

SUIT YOURSELF

Everyone has different tastes, especially when it comes to spices. If you're following a recipe and you find it too spicy, or not spicy enough, simply adjust the quantities to suit your own taste.

ADD SOME ZING

The acidic zing from a squeeze of lemon juice will enhance the flavour of almost any finished dish. Add it at the end, after cooking and don't overdo it – you want just a hint of sharpness which gives the food a fresh, clean taste.

EAT THE SEASONS

Getting fruit and veg as fresh as possible means they'll also be at their most flavoursome. Try to eat veg when it's in season and, if possible, locally grown. You will notice the difference.

Fish & seafood

MOROCCAN FISH TAGINE WITH LEMON COUSCOUS

A spicy, fragrant stew of cod, onions, peppers and tomatoes, with a hint of sweetness from dried apricots.

SERVES 4

PREP TIME 10 minutes **COOK TIME** 25 minutes

INGREDIENTS
Calorie controlled cooking spray
1 onion, finely sliced
1 red and 1 green pepper, deseeded and finely sliced
2 garlic cloves, finely sliced
1 tablespoon harissa paste
1 cinnamon stick
200g tin chopped tomatoes
200ml vegetable stock, made with ½ stock cube
50g dried apricots, sliced
600g skinless cod fillets, cut into large chunks
Small handful fresh coriander, chopped

FOR THE COUSCOUS
200g couscous
200ml hot vegetable stock, made with 1 stock cube
Grated zest and juice of ½ lemon

METHOD

1 Mist a large, nonstick, lidded frying pan with cooking spray. Add the onion and peppers and fry for 5 minutes until softened, adding a splash of water if necessary to prevent them burning. Add the garlic and harissa paste, then cook for 2-3 minutes.

2 Stir in the cinnamon, tomatoes, stock and apricots. Bring to the boil and simmer for 5 minutes. Season to taste.

3 Stir in the cod, cover, and simmer for 5 minutes until the fish is just cooked. Discard the cinnamon and stir in the coriander.

4 Meanwhile, prepare the couscous. Put the couscous in a heatproof bowl, pour over the stock and let stand for 5 minutes until the liquid has been absorbed. Fluff up the grains with a fork and stir in the lemon zest and juice.

5 Serve the couscous topped with the tagine.

7 SmartPoints
7 per serving

CUMIN-SPICED SCRAMBLED EGGS WITH SMOKED SALMON

Cumin seeds transform these scrambled eggs into something special that's perfect for brunch.

SERVES 4

PREP TIME 5 minutes **COOK TIME** 10 minutes

INGREDIENTS
Calorie controlled cooking spray
2 banana shallots, finely chopped
8 eggs
4 tablespoons skimmed milk
2 teaspoons cumin seeds
2 garlic cloves, crushed
4 multiseeded flatbreads
160g smoked salmon
Fresh coriander leaves and lemon wedges, to serve

METHOD

1 Lightly mist a large nonstick frying pan with cooking spray and set over a medium heat. Add most of the shallots and cook for 3-4 minutes until softened but not coloured.

2 Meanwhile, whisk the eggs and milk in a jug with the cumin and garlic. Pour into the frying pan and cook, stirring, for 3-4 minutes until softly scrambled. Remove the pan from the heat.

3 Toast the flatbreads and divide between plates. Top with the scrambled eggs and smoked salmon. Serve garnished with the coriander and lemon wedges, the remaining shallots and a sprinkling of freshly ground black pepper.

SmartPoints
5 per serving

Tip
Toasting the cumin seeds in a dry pan over a medium heat for a minute or two will bring out their flavour. Follow the method on page 11.

SALMON TERIYAKI BURGER WITH WASABI MAYONNAISE

This is no ordinary fish burger! Ginger, wasabi and salmon provide plenty of Japanese-inspired flavour.

SERVES 4

PREP TIME 30 minutes **COOK TIME** 4-6 minutes

INGREDIENTS

400g skinless salmon fillet, roughly chopped
1 spring onion, trimmed and thinly sliced
2cm piece fresh ginger, grated
1 small garlic clove, crushed
2 teaspoons reduced-salt soy sauce
2 teaspoons clear honey
Calorie controlled cooking spray
2 tablespoons 0% fat natural Greek yogurt
1 tablespoon reduced-fat mayonnaise
¼ teaspoon wasabi paste
4 x 70g white bread rolls, split
2 carrots, sliced into ribbons
1 cucumber, sliced into ribbons
1 small or ½ large avocado, peeled, stone removed, and thinly sliced

METHOD

1 In a food processor, pulse the salmon to a coarse paste. Transfer to a large bowl, add the spring onion, ginger and garlic, then season to taste. Mix well using your hands. Divide into 4 equal portions and shape each into an 8cm patty.

2 Put the soy sauce and honey in a microwave-safe bowl and cook on high for 10 seconds until the honey melts. Stir to combine.

3 Preheat the grill to high. Line a baking sheet with foil and mist with cooking spray. Put the patties on the prepared tray and brush with some of the soy sauce mixture. Grill for 2-3 minutes, turning once and brushing with the remaining soy sauce mixture, until cooked through.

4 Meanwhile, in a bowl, combine the yogurt, mayonnaise and wasabi paste.

5 Lightly toast the rolls, then spread the bottom halves with the wasabi mayonnaise. Top with the carrot, cucumber, salmon patties, avocado and the other halves of the rolls, and serve.

9 SmartPoints
9 per serving

Tip
You can freeze the patties for up to 2 months. Wrap individually in clingfilm and foil to freeze, then defrost in the fridge overnight and cook as in step 3.

PRAWN, CHILLI & TOMATO LINGUINE

The flavour of the prawns really shines through in this pasta dish, with the chilli adding a hint of heat.

SERVES 4

PREP TIME 5 minutes **COOK TIME** 10 minutes

INGREDIENTS
250g linguine
Calorie controlled cooking spray
1 garlic clove, crushed
1 red chilli, deseeded and finely chopped
335g cherry tomatoes, halved
350g cooked peeled king prawns
Zest and juice of 1 lemon
1 tablespoon extra-virgin olive oil
1 tablespoon finely chopped fresh flat-leaf parsley, to serve

7 SmartPoints
7 per serving

METHOD

1 Put the linguine in a large pan of salted boiling water. Bring back to the boil and simmer for 6-7 minutes, or until the linguine is al dente. Drain, reserving a little of the pasta cooking water.

2 Meanwhile, mist a large nonstick frying pan with cooking spray, add the garlic and chilli and cook over a medium heat for 1-2 minutes. Add the tomatoes and cook for another 3-4 minutes until they begin to break down. Stir in the prawns, lemon juice and olive oil until combined.

3 Add a couple of tablespoons of the reserved pasta water to the sauce, then add the cooked linguine, tossing everything together until well combined.

4 Divide between bowls and serve garnished with the lemon zest and parsley.

Tip
Try this recipe with 2 x 170g tins white crab meat in brine, drained, instead of the prawns. The SmartPoints will be the same.

THAI-SPICED MUSSELS IN COCONUT CHILLI BROTH

This fragrant seafood soup teams Thai flavours with fresh mussels in a delicious coconut broth.

SERVES 2

PREP TIME 20 minutes **COOK TIME** 10 minutes

INGREDIENTS

500g fresh mussels
Small handful fresh coriander, leaves picked and stalks reserved
Small handful fresh mint, leaves picked
2 teaspoons vegetable oil
2 spring onions, trimmed and sliced on the diagonal
2 garlic cloves, crushed
½ red chilli, finely sliced
3cm-piece fresh ginger, grated
1 lemongrass stalk
400ml tin reduced-fat coconut milk
150ml fish stock, made with ½ stock cube
2 teaspoons light brown soft sugar
2 tablespoons fish sauce
Grated zest and juice of 1 lime

SmartPoints
12 per serving

METHOD

1 Scrub the mussels, tug away any beards and discard any that are cracked or don't close when tapped gently on the kitchen counter. Roughly chop the coriander and mint leaves; then chop the coriander stalks.

2 In a large nonstick pan, heat the oil over a medium heat and fry the spring onions, garlic, chilli and ginger for 1-2 minutes. Add the coriander stalks and reduce the heat to low.

3 Meanwhile, trim the lemongrass and peel and discard the tough outermost layer. Bash with a rolling pin, then chop finely and add to the pan.

4 Stir in the coconut milk, stock, sugar, fish sauce and lime zest and juice. Bring to the boil then reduce the heat and add the mussels. Cover with a lid and cook for 3-4 minutes, until the mussels have opened. Discard any that remain shut. Stir through the coriander and mint leaves, then divide between bowls and serve.

SUMAC BAKED FISH IN A BAG

Tangy, citrusy sumac is a classic Middle-Eastern spice that is a natural match for cod in this simple recipe.

SERVES 4

PREP TIME 15 minutes **COOK TIME** 10 minutes

INGREDIENTS
200g couscous
2 spring onions, trimmed and finely sliced
Finely grated zest and slices of 1 lemon
½ teaspoon ground cumin
1 teaspoon sumac, plus extra to serve
150g cherry tomatoes, halved
1 tablespoon finely chopped fresh flat-leaf parsley
1 tablespoon finely chopped coriander, plus extra leaves to serve
4 skinless cod fillets

METHOD

1 Preheat the oven to 200°C, fan 180°C, gas mark 6. Put the couscous in a heatproof bowl with the spring onions, lemon zest, cumin and ½ teaspoon of the sumac. Pour over 250ml boiling water, cover and set aside to stand for 5 minutes. When the liquid has absorbed, fluff the couscous up with a fork and stir in the tomatoes, parsley and coriander. Season to taste.

2 Cut a 40cm square of baking paper. Put a quarter of the couscous on one half of the square and top with one of the cod fillets. Top the fish with a couple of lemon slices and sprinkle over a quarter of the remaining sumac, then season well. Seal the parcel by bringing together the edges of the paper above the fish and fold the edges from one end to the other, twisting the ends like a cracker. Repeat with the remaining couscous and cod fillets to make three more parcels, then put them onto a baking sheet.

3 Bake for 8-10 minutes or until the fish is cooked through and flakes with a fork. Serve garnished with extra sumac and coriander.

5
SmartPoints
5 per serving

CHILLI PRAWNS & CHORIZO RICE BOWL

Smoky, savoury chorizo goes so well with the prawns in this simple but satisfying rice dish.

SERVES 4

PREP TIME 5 minutes **COOK TIME** 25 minutes

INGREDIENTS

225g brown rice
1 vegetable stock cube
2 teaspoons olive oil
25g diced chorizo
200g raw peeled king prawns
1 garlic clove, thinly sliced
1 red chilli, deseeded and chopped
Small handful fresh flat-leaf parsley, chopped
1 small cucumber, peeled, deseeded and cut into sticks

 SmartPoints
7 per serving

GF See page 6

METHOD

1 Put the rice in a large pan and crumble in the stock cube, then fill the pan with water, bring to the boil and cook over a medium heat for 25 minutes, or until the rice is tender.

2 Meanwhile, heat the oil in a frying pan over a medium heat and cook the chorizo for 1 minute. Stir in the prawns and cook until just turning pink.

3 Add the garlic and chilli and continue to cook for 2 minutes, or until the prawns are fully cooked.

4 Stir through the cooked rice and half of the chopped parsley, then serve in bowls, garnished with the remaining chopped parsley and the cucumber.

SALMON FILLETS WITH A GINGER & LEMONGRASS CRUST

Topping fish fillets with a tasty crust is an easy way to give them a more interesting texture and flavour.

SERVES 4

PREP TIME 20 minutes **COOK TIME** 15 minutes

INGREDIENTS

½ lemongrass stalk, outer layer removed and the rest very finely chopped
5cm piece fresh ginger, grated
1 garlic clove, crushed
1 tablespoon finely chopped coriander, plus extra to serve
1 teaspoon olive oil
20g panko breadcrumbs
4 skinless salmon fillets
Calorie controlled cooking spray
300g Tenderstem broccoli
3 pak choi, quartered
½ tablespoon soy sauce
1 tablespoon oyster sauce
150g frozen peas
2 x 250g packs microwave brown basmati and wild rice

SmartPoints
7 per serving

METHOD

1 Preheat the oven to 200°C, fan 180°C, gas mark 6. Mix the lemongrass, ginger, garlic, coriander, olive oil and breadcrumbs together and season well. Put the salmon fillets onto a baking sheet lined with baking paper and top with the panko crust. Mist with cooking spray and bake for 12-15 minutes until cooked through.

2 Meanwhile, cook the broccoli in a pan of boiling water for 2 minutes, then add the pak choi for another 2 minutes. Remove all the veg with a slotted spoon, keeping the water, and toss with the soy and oyster sauces.

3 Add the peas to the boiling water and cook for 2-3 minutes until tender. Meanwhile, microwave the rice to pack instructions, then stir the peas into the rice. Spoon onto plates, then top with the salmon and serve with the broccoli and pak choi.

PAPRIKA FISH & FENNEL STEW

The slight aniseed flavour of fennel is great paired with white fish, while paprika adds a smoky spiciness.

SERVES 4

PREP TIME 10 minutes **COOK TIME** 20 minutes

INGREDIENTS
1 tablespoon olive oil
1 onion, finely chopped
1 large fennel bulb, finely sliced, fronds reserved
2 garlic cloves, crushed
1½ teaspoons sweet smoked paprika
750ml hot fish stock, made with 1½ stock cubes
500g passata
250g skinless cod fillets, cut into chunks
180g raw peeled king prawns
1 tablespoon finely chopped fresh flat-leaf parsley
Juice of ½ lemon
4 x 50g crusty white bread rolls, to serve

METHOD
1 Heat the oil in a medium pan and cook the onion and fennel over a medium heat for 6-8 minutes until soft, then add the garlic and paprika for another minute.

2 Add the fish stock and passata, season to taste and bring to a simmer. Turn the heat down, add the cod and prawns and cook for 3-4 minutes until just cooked through, then stir in the parsley and lemon juice. Serve topped with the reserved fennel fronds and the bread rolls on the side.

SmartPoints
6 per serving

THAI YELLOW FISH CURRY

An easy fish curry that uses a ready-made curry paste, plus plenty of fresh vegetables.

SERVES 4

PREP TIME 10 minutes **COOK TIME** 10 minutes

INGREDIENTS

Calorie controlled cooking spray
1 onion, thickly sliced
3cm piece piece fresh ginger, grated
2 tablespoons yellow curry paste
250ml reduced-fat coconut milk
250ml fish stock, made with ½ stock cube
115g baby corn, halved lengthways
1 red pepper, deseeded and sliced
500g firm white skinless fish fillets, cut into chunks
150g mange tout
Large handful fresh Thai basil leaves (if you can't find Thai basil, use regular), half roughly torn, half left whole
480g cooked brown rice, to serve
1 lime, cut into wedges, to serve (optional)

METHOD

1 Heat a large nonstick wok or frying pan over a medium-high heat. Mist with cooking spray and stir-fry the onion and ginger for 2-3 minutes or until just tender. Add the curry paste and stir-fry for 1 minute or until fragrant.

2 Add the coconut milk, fish stock, baby corn, pepper and fish. Reduce the heat to low, cover and simmer for 4-5 minutes or until the fish is cooked through. Stir in the mange tout and the torn basil leaves.

3 Serve the curry garnished with the whole basil leaves, and the rice and lime wedges, if using, on the side.

9 SmartPoints
SmartPoints value
9 per serving

Chicken & turkey

DUKKAH-CRUSTED CHICKEN WITH ROAST VEG

Dukkah is a blend of spices, crushed nuts and seeds, that makes a great coating for chicken.

SERVES 4

PREP TIME 15 minutes **COOK TIME** 40 minutes

INGREDIENTS

400g butternut squash, peeled, deseeded and cut into chunks
2 large carrots, cut into chunks
1 red onion, cut into thick wedges
1 fennel bulb, cut into thick wedges
½ teaspoon each ground cinnamon, ground cumin and ground coriander
½ tablespoon olive oil
4 tablespoons dukkah
8 x 85g skinless chicken thigh fillets
Calorie controlled cooking spray
100g kale, shredded
100g 0% fat natural Greek yogurt
Juice of 1 lemon

METHOD

1 Preheat the oven to 200°C, fan 180°C, gas mark 6. Put the butternut squash, carrots, onion and fennel on a large baking tray. Mix the ground spices together and sprinkle over the vegetables. Drizzle with the olive oil, season well and use your hands to toss everything together. Roast for 35-40 minutes, or until the vegetables are tender and golden.

2 Meanwhile, spread the dukkah out on a large plate. Mist the chicken thighs with cooking spray, then press each one into the dukkah so that one side of each fillet is well coated. Transfer to a roasting tin, coated-side up, and roast alongside the veg for 20 minutes, or until cooked through.

3 Just before the chicken and vegetables are ready, put the kale in a microwave-safe bowl, cover with clingfilm and microwave at full power for 1 minute 30 seconds until wilted. Toss the wilted kale through the roasted vegetables.

4 In a small bowl, whisk together the yogurt and lemon juice and season to taste.

5 Serve the roasted vegetables and chicken with the lemon yogurt on the side.

 **SmartPoints**
10 per serving

 See page 6

HARISSA CHICKEN SKEWERS WITH BULGUR WHEAT SALAD

These healthier kebabs are served with a fresh-tasting bulgur wheat salad, flavoured with toasted cumin.

SERVES 4

PREP TIME 10 minutes **COOK TIME** 10 minutes

INGREDIENTS

2 tablespoons harissa paste
80g fat-free natural yogurt, plus extra for serving
400g skinless chicken breast fillets, diced
1 courgette, thickly sliced
1 red pepper, deseeded and cut into chunks
175g bulgur wheat
1 carrot, peeled and grated
3 tomatoes, deseeded and diced
1 red onion, finely sliced
150g peas, blanched
Large handful fresh flat-leaf parsley, chopped
40g toasted pine nuts
1 teaspoon cumin seeds, toasted in a dry frying pan and lightly crushed
1 lemon, cut into wedges, to serve

YOU WILL ALSO NEED
Bamboo or metal skewers

 SmartPoints
6 per serving

METHOD

1 If using bamboo skewers, put them in a bowl of water to soak for at least 10 minutes.

2 Heat the grill to high. Put the harissa and yogurt in a bowl with the chicken, then season and mix well. Thread onto skewers with the courgette and pepper and grill for 10 minutes, turning occasionally, until cooked through.

3 Meanwhile, cook the bulgur wheat in a pan of boiling water for 8 minutes, then drain and cool under cold running water. Stir together with the carrot, tomatoes, onion, peas, parsley, pine nuts and crushed cumin seeds. Season and serve with the skewers, a dollop of yogurt and the lemon wedges on the side.

Tip
To toast the cumin seeds follow the method on page 11, then allow to cool before crushing them using a pestle and mortar.

CHICKEN & CHIPOTLE STEW WITH QUINOA

Chilli, tomato and lime bring an unmistakably Mexican flavour to this delicious stew.

SERVES 4

PREP TIME 10 minutes **COOK TIME** 35 minutes

INGREDIENTS

Calorie controlled cooking spray
1 onion, finely sliced
1 red and 1 orange pepper, each deseeded and sliced
2 garlic cloves, crushed
250g mushrooms, sliced
1 tablespoon chipotle paste
1 tablespoon red wine vinegar
2 x 400g tins chopped tomatoes
1 teaspoon caster sugar
1 tablespoon tomato purée
2 teaspoons ground cumin
¼ teaspoon paprika
¼ teaspoon cayenne pepper
70g quinoa
2 x 165g skinless chicken breast fillets
Large handful fresh coriander, chopped
Juice of 1 lime
4 tablespoons reduced-fat soured cream, to serve

METHOD

1 Mist a large pan with cooking spray and put over a medium heat. Add the onion and peppers and cook for 3-4 minutes until starting to soften. You may have to add a splash of water to stop the mixture catching.

2 Add the garlic and mushrooms and cook for 3-4 minutes until golden. Stir in the chipotle paste and cook for a further minute.

3 Add the vinegar and tomatoes, then fill one of the tins with water and add to the pan with the sugar, tomato purée, cumin, paprika, cayenne pepper and quinoa. Season to taste.

4 Put the chicken in the pan and push it under the sauce until submerged. Cover and simmer for 20 minutes, or until the chicken and quinoa are cooked through.

5 Once the chicken is cooked, remove the stew from the heat and transfer the chicken to a board. Using 2 forks, shred the meat and return to the pan with the coriander and lime juice.

6 Ladle the stew into bowls and serve with the soured cream.

3 SmartPoints value

SmartPoints
3 per serving

 GF See page 6

MISO ROAST CHICKEN

Chicken drumsticks are coated in a Japanese-style marinade and roasted to sticky perfection.

SERVES 4

PREP TIME 15 minutes + marinating **COOK TIME** 55 minutes

INGREDIENTS

2 tablespoons miso paste
1 tablespoon mirin
2cm piece fresh ginger, chopped
2 teaspoons clear honey
1 teaspoon sesame oil
3 tablespoons dark soy sauce
8 x 105g chicken drumsticks, skin removed
1 whole cauliflower, leaves and core removed, florets chopped
Calorie controlled cooking spray
1 carrot, finely diced
75g frozen petits pois, thawed
2 garlic cloves, crushed
1 egg, beaten
3 spring onions, trimmed and sliced

SmartPoints
4 per serving

GF See page 6

METHOD

1 Combine the miso paste, mirin, ginger, honey, sesame oil and 2 tablespoons of the soy sauce in a bowl. Put the chicken in a roasting tin, pour over the marinade and turn to coat. Cover with clingfilm and chill for 30 minutes to marinate.

2 Preheat the oven to 180°C, fan 160°C, gas mark 4. Roast the chicken for 55 minutes, turning and basting now and then, until cooked.

3 When the drumsticks are halfway through cooking, grate the cauliflower on the largest plane of a grater or blitz in a food processor until it resembles rice.

4 Mist a nonstick wok with cooking spray and stir-fry the carrot for 4 minutes over a high heat. Add the petits pois and garlic and stir-fry for another minute. Add the cauliflower and cook for 3-4 minutes, until the cauliflower is cooked, but not mushy.

5 Remove the cauliflower mixture from the wok and set aside. Mist the wok again with cooking spray, then pour in the egg and swirl. When the egg is set at the sides, but still runny on top, return the cauliflower to the wok and stir quickly, for 1-2 minutes, scraping the sides. Drizzle over the rest of the soy sauce, then season, and stir to combine. Remove from the heat, then stir in the spring onions and serve with the chicken drumsticks.

CAJUN CHICKEN PITTAS

Tasty spiced chicken, red pepper and onion in a toasted pitta bread makes a speedy, satisfying lunch.

SERVES 2

PREP TIME 10 minutes **COOK TIME** 12 minutes

INGREDIENTS
2 x 165g skinless chicken breast fillets
Calorie controlled cooking spray
2 teaspoons Cajun seasoning
2 white pitta breads
2 tablespoons reduced-fat mayonnaise
Juice of ½ lime
1 small garlic clove, crushed
Handful shredded iceberg lettuce
1 small red pepper, deseeded and sliced
½ red onion, finely chopped

METHOD

1 Mist the chicken breast fillets with cooking spray and sprinkle over the Cajun seasoning. Mist a nonstick frying pan with cooking spray and put over a medium heat. Add the chicken and cook for 10-12 minutes, turning occasionally, or until the chicken is cooked through. Allow to cool slightly, then use 2 forks to shred and set aside.

2 Meanwhile, cut along one edge of each pitta to make a pocket. Lightly toast, then set aside and allow to cool slightly.

3 Mix the mayonnaise with the lime juice and garlic.

4 Spread the inside of the toasted pittas with the mayonnaise and fill with the shredded chicken, lettuce, pepper and a sprinkling of red onion, then serve.

SmartPoints
7 per serving

Tip
Cajun seasoning is a blend of paprika, pepper, cayenne pepper, dried garlic and herbs. It's great as a rub for chicken or fish.

KOREAN CHICKEN & KIMCHI FRIED RICE

A mix of spiced and fermented vegetables, kimchi adds a unique flavour to this quick chicken fried rice.

SERVES 4

PREP TIME 5 minutes **COOK TIME** 5 minutes

INGREDIENTS

1 tablespoon vegetable oil
1 large carrot, cut into matchsticks
3 spring onions, trimmed and thinly sliced
200g Chinese leaf, shredded
250g pouch microwave brown rice
1 tablespoon chia seeds
400g cooked skinless chicken breast fillets, shredded
150g kimchi

METHOD

1 Heat a wok or large frying pan over a high heat. Add the oil and heat for 30 seconds. Stir-fry the carrot and half the spring onions for 2 minutes. Add the Chinese leaf and stir-fry for 1 minute.

2 Meanwhile, cook the rice to pack instructions, then add it to the wok along with the chia seeds, chicken and kimchi. Stir-fry for 1 minute or until hot.

3 Serve topped with the remaining spring onions.

5 SmartPoints
5 per serving

Tip

Serve this with steamed Asian greens, such as pak choi or choi sum, for no extra SmartPoints.

SPICY SZECHUAN TURKEY MINCE WITH GREEN BEANS

A quick turkey stir-fry with spicy Chinese flavours and tender green beans, served with brown rice.

SERVES 4

PREP TIME 10 minutes **COOK TIME** 25 minutes

INGREDIENTS

200g brown rice
2 teaspoons olive oil
300g green beans, trimmed
500g lean turkey breast mince
3 garlic cloves, finely chopped
3cm piece fresh ginger, chopped
1 red chilli, deseeded and chopped
¼ teaspoon Szechuan peppercorns, crushed
100g spring onions, trimmed and thinly sliced
2 tablespoons light soy sauce
2 tablespoons rice wine vinegar
1 teaspoon light brown soft sugar
1 tablespoon chilli sauce or paste

METHOD

1 Cook the rice to pack instructions, then drain and set aside.

2 Meanwhile, heat the oil in a pan over a high heat, add the beans and cook for 3 minutes, then add the turkey mince. Cook for a further 5 minutes or until the mince is cooked through.

3 Stir in the garlic, ginger, chilli, Szechuan peppercorns and half the spring onions, and continue to cook for a further 2 minutes. Add the soy sauce, rice wine vinegar, sugar and chilli sauce, and cook for 3-4 minutes.

4 Remove from the heat, stir in the remaining spring onions and serve with the rice.

 **SmartPoints**
6 per serving

 See page 6

CHICKEN JALFREZI WITH RICE

Fresh peppers, chilli and tomatoes are key ingredients in jalfrezi – this chicken version is packed with flavour.

SERVES 2

PREP TIME 10 minutes **COOK TIME** 35 minutes

INGREDIENTS
2 x 125g skinless chicken breast fillets
2 teaspoons garam masala
1 teaspoon ground coriander
1 red chilli, deseeded and finely chopped
3 garlic cloves, crushed
2cm piece fresh ginger, grated
1 teaspoon vegetable oil
1 onion, sliced
1 green pepper, deseeded and diced
400g tin chopped tomatoes
100g brown rice
Handful fresh coriander, chopped
1 tablespoon 0% fat natural Greek yogurt

METHOD

1 Make slashes in the chicken breast fillets. Mix the spices, most of the chilli, the garlic and ginger with 1 teaspoon cold water to make a paste. Rub into the chicken and set aside.

2 Heat the oil in a large pan and fry the onion for 5 minutes. Add the pepper, fry for 5 minutes, then add the chicken and cook for a further 5 minutes, turning once. Add the tomatoes with 2 tablespoons water. Cover and simmer on a low heat for 15 minutes. Remove the lid, turn the chicken and cook for 3 minutes or until the sauce is reduced.

3 Meanwhile, cook the rice to pack instructions, then stir through most of the coriander. Serve the rice and chicken, topped with the yogurt and the remaining coriander and red chilli.

SmartPoints
6 per serving

   See page 6

SUMAC CHICKEN KEBABS WITH HERBY COUSCOUS

A marinade of pomegranate molasses and sumac gives tender chicken a delicious sticky glaze.

SERVES 4

PREP TIME 10 minutes + marinating **COOK TIME** 30 minutes

INGREDIENTS

2 teaspoons olive oil
2 tablespoons pomegranate molasses
1 teaspoon sumac
500g skinless chicken breast fillets, cut into bite-size chunks

FOR THE COUSCOUS

Calorie controlled cooking spray
1 onion, finely sliced
1 teaspoon ground cinnamon
240g couscous
Pinch of saffron
350ml hot chicken stock, made with ½ stock cube
Grated zest and juice of 1 lemon
Handful fresh flat-leaf parsley, roughly chopped
Handful fresh mint leaves, roughly chopped

YOU WILL ALSO NEED

Bamboo or metal skewers

METHOD

1 To make the marinade, whisk together the olive oil, pomegranate molasses and sumac. Season to taste.

2 Put the chicken pieces in a large bowl and coat with the marinade. Cover with clingfilm and chill in the fridge for 2 hours to marinate. If using bamboo skewers, put them in a bowl of water to soak for at least 10 minutes.

3 Meanwhile, mist a large nonstick frying pan with cooking spray, then fry the onion with the ground cinnamon over a medium heat for 10-15 minutes until very soft.

4 Put the couscous in a large heatproof bowl. Add the saffron to the stock, leave for 30 seconds and pour over the couscous. Cover the bowl with a plate and leave for 10 minutes or until the stock has been fully absorbed. Stir through the cooked onion, the lemon zest and juice, and the herbs. Season to taste.

5 Heat the grill to high. Thread the chicken onto 4 large (or 8 small) skewers and cook under the grill for 12-15 minutes, turning occasionally, until cooked. Serve immediately on the couscous.

SmartPoints
8 per serving

CHICKEN & MANGO CURRY

Coconut milk and mango give this chicken curry
a delicious richness, without it feeling heavy.

SERVES 4

PREP TIME 15 minutes **COOK TIME** 35 minutes

INGREDIENTS

1 tablespoon olive oil
450g skinless chicken
breast fillets, diced
1 onion, finely chopped
1 teaspoon fennel seeds,
lightly crushed
½ teaspoon fenugreek seeds
1 teaspoon black onion seeds
1 teaspoon ground coriander
½ teaspoon ground turmeric
20 dried or fresh curry leaves
4 garlic cloves, chopped
2cm piece fresh ginger,
chopped
1 green chilli, deseeded and
finely chopped, plus extra
sliced green chilli, to garnish
1 under-ripe mango, peeled,
stone removed, and
cut into wedges
200ml reduced-fat
coconut milk
250ml hot chicken stock,
made with 1 stock cube
200g basmati rice
Squeeze of lime juice

METHOD

1 Heat half the oil in a large nonstick pan, add the chicken and
cook over a medium-high heat for 5 minutes until golden all over.
Remove with a slotted spoon and set aside.

2 Heat the remaining oil in the same pan, add the onion and a good
pinch of salt and gently cook for 10 minutes, stirring occasionally
and adding a splash of water if it starts to catch. Add the spices,
curry leaves, garlic, ginger and green chilli. Cook for 2-3 minutes
until fragrant.

3 Add the mango and pour in the coconut milk and stock. Return
the chicken to the pan and simmer for 10-15 minutes until the
chicken is cooked through.

4 Meanwhile, cook the rice to pack instructions.

5 Season the curry to taste and stir in the lime juice. Transfer to a
large serving bowl and garnish with the extra green chilli, then
serve with the rice.

SmartPoints
9 per serving

See page 6

ZA'ATAR CHICKEN DRUMSTICKS WITH TAHINI YOGURT

This Middle-Eastern style chicken dish is served with green salad leaves and a delicious yogurt dressing.

SERVES 4

PREP TIME 10 minutes **COOK TIME** 30 minutes

INGREDIENTS

2 tablespoons za'atar
2 small garlic cloves, crushed
2 teaspoons olive oil
1½ tablespoons lemon juice
8 x 105g chicken drumsticks, skin removed
100g fat-free natural yogurt
1 tablespoon tahini
Pinch ground cumin
2 x 250g packs microwave brown rice
Peppery salad leaves, to serve

10 SmartPoints
10 per serving

 See page 6

METHOD

1 Preheat the oven to 200°C, fan 180°C, gas mark 6. Mix the za'atar, half the garlic, the olive oil and 1 tablespoon of the lemon juice together in a bowl, then add the chicken. Season to taste and toss until coated. Put the chicken onto a tray lined with baking paper and bake for 30 minutes until cooked through.

2 Meanwhile, mix the yogurt, tahini, cumin and the remaining lemon juice and garlic together in a bowl until well combined, then season to taste.

3 Cook the rice according to pack instructions, then serve with the chicken, salad leaves and tahini yogurt.

> **Tip**
>
> Za'atar is a blend of herbs, spices and sesame seeds. Use it as a seasoning on chicken, fish and meat for an authentic Middle-Eastern flavour.

JERK CHICKEN TRAYBAKE WITH MANGO SALSA

An easy chicken and vegetable bake that's made extra special with a flavour-packed salsa on the side.

SERVES 4

PREP TIME 15 minutes **COOK TIME** 45 minutes

INGREDIENTS
4 skinless chicken breasts
4 tablespoons jerk cooking sauce
500g sweet potato, peeled, halved and cut into 1cm slices
Calorie controlled cooking spray
3 mixed peppers, deseeded and cut into 4cm chunks
Small bunch spring onions, trimmed and cut into 4cm pieces

FOR THE MANGO SALSA
½ mango, peeled and diced
Grated zest and juice of 1 lime
1 small red chilli, deseeded and finely chopped
½ small red onion, finely chopped
1 tablespoon fresh coriander, chopped

 SmartPoints
5 per serving

METHOD

1 Preheat the oven to 200°C, fan 180°C, gas mark 6. Put the chicken in a bowl with the jerk sauce and toss until well combined and set aside.

2 Put the sweet potato into a large roasting tin, mist with cooking spray and season to taste. Roast for 20 minutes, then nestle the peppers, spring onions and chicken among the sweet potato and cook for another 25 minutes until the chicken is cooked through and the vegetables are soft and golden.

3 Meanwhile, combine the salsa ingredients in a small bowl and serve alongside the chicken and vegetables.

Tip

Instead of jerk sauce, you could use a pouch of Weight Watchers Spicy Jerk Marinade for the same SmartPoints.

Meat

PAPRIKA BEEF & BUTTER BEAN GOULASH

The deeply-flavoured stew of beef, butter beans, peppers and tomatoes is perfect for a chilly evening.

SERVES 4

PREP TIME 20 minutes **COOK TIME** 1 hour 45 minutes

INGREDIENTS
500g lean beef braising steak, cut into chunks
Calorie controlled cooking spray
2 onions, sliced
2 garlic cloves, crushed
½ tablespoon smoked paprika
400g tin chopped tomatoes
300ml beef stock, made with ½ stock cube
1 red and 1 green pepper, each deseeded and roughly chopped
410g tin butter beans, drained and rinsed

SmartPoints
4 per serving

 See page 6

METHOD

1 Preheat the oven to 150°C, fan 130°C, gas mark 2.

2 Season the steak and mist a lidded flameproof casserole with the cooking spray. Brown half the steak over a medium heat and transfer to a plate. Repeat with the rest of the beef.

3 Mist the casserole again with a little more cooking spray and cook the onions for 5 minutes, adding a splash of water, if needed, to stop them from sticking. Once softened, stir in the garlic and smoked paprika and cook for a further minute, then add the tomatoes and beef stock. Return the beef to the casserole, season and bring to a simmer. Cover and transfer the casserole to the oven to cook for 1 hour.

4 Remove the casserole from the oven and stir in the peppers and butter beans. Replace the lid and return the casserole to the oven to cook for a further 30 minutes, or until the meat is meltingly tender and the vegetables have softened.

HARISSA PORK WITH CUMIN-SPICED 'NOODLES'

Marinated pork steaks are served on a colourful combination of sweet potatoes, carrots and rocket.

SERVES 2

PREP TIME 15 minutes + marinating **COOK TIME** 8 minutes

INGREDIENTS

1 tablespoon clear honey
3 teaspoons harissa paste
Juice of ½ lemon, plus lemon wedges to serve
2 x 100g lean pork steaks, trimmed of fat
Calorie controlled cooking spray
1 large carrot, peeled and spiralised
1 sweet potato (around 150g), peeled and spiralised
1 red onion, finely sliced
2 garlic cloves, finely chopped
½ teaspoon cumin seeds
Handful fresh coriander leaves, roughly chopped
2 teaspoons 0% fat natural Greek yogurt
Large handful rocket

 SmartPoints
9 per serving

 See page 6

METHOD

1 In a bowl, make a marinade by mixing together the honey, 2 teaspoons of the harissa paste and all of the lemon juice.

2 Put the pork between two pieces of cling film and bash with a rolling pin to flatten. Add to the bowl with the marinade and turn to coat well. Cover and set aside to marinate for 5 minutes.

3 To make the 'noodles', mist a large nonstick frying pan with cooking spray and heat over a medium heat. Add the carrot, sweet potato, onion, garlic and cumin seeds. Season to taste, add a few drops of water and cook for 5-6 minutes until the sweet potato is tender but retains some bite. Add a little more water if it starts to catch. Stir in the chopped coriander and cook for another minute.

4 Meanwhile, mist a nonstick griddle pan with cooking spray and heat over a medium heat. Season the pork all over and griddle for 6-8 minutes, turning once, until cooked through. In a small bowl, combine the remaining harissa paste and the yogurt with a splash of water to make a thin dressing.

5 Add the rocket and the yogurt dressing to the 'noodles' and toss to wilt the rocket slightly, then divide between plates. Top with the pork steaks and serve with the lemon wedges for squeezing.

LAMB TIKKA KEBABS WITH LENTILS & SPICY COLESLAW

Mango chutney is the secret ingredient in the marinade for these kebabs, served with a chilli-spiced coleslaw.

SERVES 4

PREP TIME 15 minutes + marinating **COOK TIME** 20 minutes

INGREDIENTS
400g diced lean lamb leg steak
4 tablespoons fat-free natural yogurt
2 tablespoons mango chutney
1½ tablespoons tikka curry powder
150g dried green or Puy lentils
2 small red onions, each cut into 8 thin wedges
200g cherry tomatoes

FOR THE SPICY COLESLAW
1 orange, peeled and segmented (reserve the juice)
¼ red cabbage, finely shredded
3 spring onions, trimmed and chopped
¼ red chilli, deseeded and finely diced
2 tablespoons fresh mint leaves, chopped, plus a few leaves to garnish

YOU WILL ALSO NEED
Bamboo or metal skewers

 **SmartPoints**
8 per serving

GF See page 6

METHOD

1 Put the lamb in a non-metallic bowl. Stir in the yogurt, chutney and curry powder, then season with salt and freshly ground black pepper. Set aside to marinate for at least 15 minutes. If using bamboo skewers, put them in a bowl of water to soak for at least 10 minutes.

2 Meanwhile, cook the lentils to pack instructions. For the coleslaw, combine all of the ingredients, including the orange juice, in a bowl and season well.

3 Preheat the grill to medium-high. Thread the lamb, onions and tomatoes onto 8 skewers. Grill for 15-20 minutes, turning occasionally, until cooked through and lightly charred.

4 Serve the kebabs with the lentils and coleslaw, garnished with the mint leaves.

Tip
You could also serve this with 1 wholemeal pitta bread per person, for an extra 4 SmartPoints per serving.

SAUSAGE SHAKSHUKA WITH FETA

This dish of eggs poached in a tomato sauce with sausages makes a great breakfast or lunch.

SERVES 4

PREP TIME 10 minutes **COOK TIME** 35 minutes

INGREDIENTS

1 tablespoon sunflower oil
6 reduced-fat sausages, halved
1 onion, thinly sliced
1 red pepper, chopped
1½ teaspoons paprika
1 teaspoon dried oregano
400g tin chopped tomatoes with garlic
4 eggs
100g lighter feta
Small handful fresh flat-leaf parsley, roughly chopped

SmartPoints
5 per serving

METHOD

1 Heat the oil in a large, deep lidded frying pan over a medium-high heat, then add the sausage halves. Fry for 5 minutes on each side until cooked through and brown. Transfer to a plate and cover with kitchen foil to keep warm.

2 Reduce the heat to medium and add the onion and red pepper to the pan. Stir-fry for 5 minutes, then add the paprika and oregano and cook for another 2 minutes until fragrant. Add the chopped tomatoes and season to taste. Fill one-third of the empty tin with water and add to the pan. Mix well and gently simmer for 10 minutes.

3 Return the sausages to the pan, nestling them into the sauce, then make 4 wells with a spoon and crack an egg into each one. Cover the pan with the lid and let the eggs poach in the sauce for 5-6 minutes. Crumble the feta over the eggs, then scatter over the chopped parsley and a sprinkling of black pepper and serve.

THAI PORK CURRY WITH COCONUT NOODLES

Using a ready-made Thai red curry paste makes this tasty dish super simple and speedy.

SERVES 4

PREP TIME 10 minutes **COOK TIME** 15 minutes

INGREDIENTS

2 tablespoons Thai red curry paste
4 x 100g pork escalopes
1 teaspoon olive oil
400g pak choi, halved
150g flat instant rice noodles
150ml reduced-fat coconut milk
¼ teaspoon caster sugar
Juice of 1 lime
4 spring onions, trimmed and sliced
Small handful fresh coriander, chopped
1 red chilli, deseeded and finely sliced
1 tablespoon fish sauce
1 tablespoon soy sauce

SmartPoints
9 per serving

METHOD

1 Brush or rub the curry paste over the pork. Heat a griddle pan to high and brush with a little of the oil. Griddle the pork for 2-3 minutes on each side, or until golden and cooked through. Remove and let rest for 5 minutes.

2 Meanwhile, add the remaining oil to the pan and cook the pak choi for 1-2 minutes, cut side down, until golden. Turn and add 200ml boiling water to the pan. Cover and cook for a further 2 minutes until tender.

3 Meanwhile, put the noodles in a heatproof bowl and pour over enough boiling water to cover them. Leave for 3 minutes, then drain and rinse under cold running water.

4 In a small pan, heat the coconut milk with the caster sugar, lime juice, spring onions, coriander, chilli, fish sauce and soy sauce to a gentle simmer.

5 Cut the pork into strips. Serve the noodles in bowls with the coconut sauce poured over, topped with the pak choi and pork.

SMOKY BLACK BEAN & CHORIZO SOUP

Chorizo and paprika give this easy soup a spicy, smoky flavour, with avocado and coriander adding freshness.

SERVES 4

PREP TIME 15 minutes **COOK TIME** 25 minutes

INGREDIENTS
2 teaspoons olive oil
1 red onion, finely chopped
3 celery sticks, finely chopped
115g chorizo, diced
3 garlic cloves, crushed
½ teaspoon chilli flakes
1 teaspoon smoked paprika
2 x 400g tins black beans, drained and rinsed
400g tin chopped tomatoes
750ml chicken stock, made with 1 reduced-salt stock cube
2 teaspoons lime juice
½ small avocado, peeled, stone removed and flesh chopped
Handful fresh coriander leaves, larger ones chopped
1 red chilli, finely sliced

METHOD

1 Heat the oil in a large pan over a medium heat. Cook the onion and celery, stirring, for 5 minutes or until softened. Add the chorizo, garlic, chilli flakes and paprika and cook, stirring occasionally, for 3 minutes or until the chorizo is golden.

2 Add the beans, tomatoes and stock and bring to a boil. Reduce the heat to a simmer, partially cover, and cook for 15 minutes. Set aside to cool slightly.

3 Transfer half the soup to a blender or food processor, and blitz until smooth. Return to the pan and reheat over a medium-low heat until hot. Stir through the lime juice and season to taste.

4 Ladle into bowls and serve topped with the avocado, coriander and chilli.

 **SmartPoints**
6 per serving

  See page 6

QUICK LAMB BIRYANI

This all-in-one Indian classic is packed with flavour and on the table in just 20 minutes.

SERVES 4

PREP TIME 5 minutes **COOK TIME** 15 minutes

INGREDIENTS

Calorie controlled cooking spray
400g diced lean lamb leg
1 onion, sliced
1 garlic clove, finely chopped
40g medium-hot curry paste, such as rogan josh
250g pack microwave basmati rice
1 teaspoon ground turmeric
1 teaspoon garam masala
200g broccoli, cut into small florets
100g young leaf spinach
Juice of 1 lemon
5g toasted flaked almonds
75g tzatziki

METHOD

1 Mist a large nonstick pan with cooking spray and place over a high heat. Add the lamb and fry for 5 minutes, until just browned. Add the onion and fry for a further 5 minutes, stirring in the garlic and curry paste for the last minute.

2 Add the rice, 3 tablespoons water and the spices. Cook, stirring, over a high heat for 3-4 minutes.

3 Meanwhile, bring a pan of water to the boil and cook the broccoli florets for 3-4 minutes, until just tender. Drain and gently stir into the rice mixture along with the spinach and lemon juice. Cook for 1 minute until the spinach has just wilted.

4 Serve garnished with the almonds, with the tzatziki on the side.

9 **SmartPoints**
9 per serving

GF See page 6

SPICED BEEF NACHOS

Everyone will love these nachos – they're quick and easy to put together, with plenty of Tex-Mex flavour.

SERVES 2

PREP TIME 10 minutes **COOK TIME** 15 minutes

INGREDIENTS
Calorie controlled cooking spray
1 onion, finely chopped
1 garlic clove, crushed
1 green chilli, finely chopped
250g extra lean 5% fat beef mince
Handful fresh coriander, chopped
Juice of 1 lime
60g quark
¼ iceberg lettuce, shredded
30g low-fat cheese, grated
100g tomatoes, sliced
Chopped jalapeño chillies, to garnish (optional)

FOR THE NACHOS
2 Weight Watchers Wraps, cut into small triangles
Calorie controlled cooking spray
¼ teaspoon smoked paprika
¼ teaspoon garlic granules

METHOD

1 Mist a nonstick pan with cooking spray and set over a medium heat. Cook the onion, garlic and chilli for 5 minutes. Add the mince and cook for 10 minutes, until cooked through. Stir in half the coriander, then season.

2 Meanwhile, make the nachos. Preheat the oven to 180°C, fan 160°C, gas mark 4. Spread the wrap triangles out onto a large baking sheet in a single layer. Mist with cooking spray, sprinkle over the paprika and garlic granules, then bake for 8 minutes, until crisp.

3 In a small bowl, combine the lime juice, quark and remaining coriander. Serve the nachos topped with the spiced mince, lettuce, cheese, tomatoes and quark mixture. Garnish with the jalapeños, if using.

9 SmartPoints
9 per serving

BOBOTIE

Lightly spiced beef mince curry is topped with a savoury custard in this popular South African dish.

SERVES 6

PREP TIME 10 minutes **COOK TIME** 1 hour 15 minutes

INGREDIENTS

80g wholemeal bread, crusts removed
300ml skimmed milk
4 bay leaves
Calorie controlled cooking spray
1 large onion, finely chopped
2 garlic cloves, crushed
1kg extra-lean 5% fat beef mince
4 teaspoons curry powder
1 tablespoon Worcestershire sauce
2 tablespoons mango chutney
1 beef stock cube, crumbled
½ tablespoon cornflour
2 large eggs
70g rocket

SmartPoints
8 per serving

METHOD

1 Preheat the oven to 180°C, fan 160°C, gas mark 4. Soak the bread in the milk with 2 of the bay leaves and set aside.

2 Mist a large, deep nonstick frying pan with cooking spray, put over a medium heat and fry the onion for 6-8 minutes until soft, then add the garlic for another minute. Add the beef and fry for 4-5 minutes until browned.

3 Stir in the curry powder, Worcestershire sauce, mango chutney, remaining bay leaves and stock cube. Season to taste and mix well. Cook for 10 minutes, then squeeze the milk out of the bread (reserve the milk) and stir the bread into the meat until well combined. Pour the meat mixture into a baking dish (remove and discard the bay leaves), and level the surface with a spatula.

4 Put the cornflour into a small bowl and pour over a splash of the reserved milk, whisking until combined, then pour the mixture back into the milk with the eggs and lightly whisk until just combined. Season to taste and pour it over the meat mixture, leaving the bay leaves from the milk on the top. Bake for 35-40 minutes until the top is set and golden, then serve with the rocket.

Tip
You could also serve this with steamed spinach and 300g boiled baby potatoes, for an extra 1 SmartPoint per serving.

STICKY BOURBON PORK

A smoky, barbecue-style marinade brings a taste of the American south to these tempting pork skewers.

SERVES 4

PREP TIME 15 minutes + marinating **COOK TIME** 10 minutes

INGREDIENTS
500g lean pork tenderloin fillet, cut into large chunks
1 red onion, cut into wedges
Chopped fresh flat-leaf parsley leaves, to garnish

FOR THE MARINADE
3 tablespoons maple syrup
3 tablespoons bourbon
2 tablespoons Worcestershire sauce
2 teaspoons smoked paprika
Grated zest of 1 orange
2 garlic cloves, crushed

FOR THE BUTTERMILK SLAW
¼ red cabbage, finely shredded
¼ white cabbage, finely shredded
2 carrots, grated
1 red onion, finely sliced
4 tablespoons buttermilk
3 tablespoons reduced-fat mayonnaise
1 tablespoon cider vinegar

YOU WILL ALSO NEED
Bamboo or metal skewers

SmartPoints
8 per serving

METHOD

1 To make the marinade, combine all the marinade ingredients in a bowl. Season to taste and add the pork. Stir to coat, cover, then marinate in the fridge for at least 4 hours, or preferably overnight. If using bamboo skewers, put them in a bowl of water to soak for at least 10 minutes

2 Bring the pork to room temperature, then thread onto 8 skewers, alternating with the onion wedges. Reserve the marinade.

3 Season the skewers to taste and cook on a hot barbecue or griddle pan for 8-10 minutes, turning frequently and brushing with the reserved marinade. Remove from the heat and rest for 5 minutes.

4 Meanwhile, make the buttermilk slaw. Put all the vegetables in a serving bowl. Mix the buttermilk, mayonnaise and cider vinegar together in a small jug and stir through the vegetables.

5 Serve the skewers on the slaw, garnished with the chopped parsley.

ASIAN SPICED BROTH WITH PORK BALLS & CABBAGE

This tempting bowl of pork meatballs and vegetables in a fragrant broth is topped with a boiled egg.

SERVES 4

PREP TIME 20 minutes **COOK TIME** 20 minutes

INGREDIENTS
400g 5% fat pork mince
3 garlic cloves, finely chopped
4cm piece fresh ginger, grated
¼ teaspoon ground Szechuan peppercorns
Pinch chilli flakes
¼ teaspoon ground cumin
1 teaspoon olive oil
4 eggs
Calorie controlled cooking spray
1 lemongrass stalk, outer layer removed and the rest chopped
2 red chillies, finely chopped, plus extra to garnish
1.2 litres chicken stock, made with 1 stock cube
1 star anise
250g mushrooms, sliced
150g Savoy cabbage, shredded
150g broccoli, cut into florets
2 tablespoons soy sauce
1½ teaspoons fish sauce
2 teaspoons hot pepper sauce
Juice of 1 lime
3 spring onions, trimmed and sliced

METHOD

1 Mix the pork mince with half the garlic and ginger and all the peppercorns, chilli flakes and cumin. Divide into 20 balls.

2 Heat the oil in a deep nonstick pan and cook the balls, in batches, for 5-10 minutes. Remove and set aside.

3 Meanwhile, cook the eggs in boiling water for 7 minutes. Remove, run under cold water for a minute, peel and halve.

4 Mist the pork pan with cooking spray and cook the remaining garlic and ginger with the lemongrass and chilli for 2 minutes. Add the stock with the star anise, bring to the boil, then turn down to a gentle simmer.

5 Add the mushrooms, cabbage and broccoli, then return the meatballs to the pan. Cook for 5 minutes or until the meatballs are cooked through. Season with the soy, fish and hot pepper sauces and lime juice. Serve with the eggs in the soup and the spring onions and extra chilli scattered over.

4 SmartPoints
SmartPoints value
4 per serving

GF See page 6

Tip
Try using a combination of mushrooms, such as oyster and shiitake, in this dish.

PIRI PIRI PORK WITH ROASTED PEPPER RICE

This impressive looking dish is a great choice for entertaining, and is simple to put together.

SERVES 4

PREP TIME 20 minutes + marinating & resting **COOK TIME** 1 hour

INGREDIENTS
3 red chillies, deseeded and finely chopped
3 garlic cloves, finely sliced
1 teaspoon dried oregano
1 teaspoon dried tarragon
2 teaspoons smoked sweet paprika
2 tablespoons chopped fresh flat-leaf parsley
Juice of 2 lemons
1 teaspoon salt
500g lean pork fillet, trimmed of fat

FOR THE RICE
4 mixed peppers
2 garlic cloves, unpeeled
Calorie controlled cooking spray
2 x 250g packs microwave brown rice
Large handful of fresh flat-leaf parsley, roughly chopped

METHOD

1 Put the chillies, garlic, oregano, tarragon, paprika, parsley, lemon juice and salt in a food processor and pulse to form a paste. Spread all over the pork fillet, cover and marinate in the fridge for at least 2 hours, or preferably overnight.

2 Preheat the oven to 200°C, fan 180°C, gas mark 6. To make the rice, put the peppers and garlic in a roasting tray and mist with cooking spray. Season and roast for 25-30 minutes, until the skin starts to blacken and blister. Remove from the oven and transfer to a heatproof bowl. Cover with clingfilm and set aside until the peppers are cool enough to handle. When cooled, peel off the skin and remove the seeds. Roughly chop the flesh and put in a bowl. Squeeze the garlic from its skin and mix through the peppers.

3 Remove the pork from the fridge and put in a roasting tin. Roast for 25-30 minutes, until cooked through. Remove from the oven and set aside to rest for 10-15 minutes, covered with kitchen foil.

4 Meanwhile, cook the rice to pack instructions, then add to the bowl with the peppers and garlic. Add the parsley and mix well.

5 Cut the pork into 12 thick slices, then serve with the rice.

 **SmartPoints**
10 per serving

 See page 6

Veggie

SPICED NASI GORENG

Originally from Indonesia, this spicy rice and vegetable dish is topped with a soft poached egg.

SERVES 4

PREP TIME 25 minutes **COOK TIME** 20 minutes

INGREDIENTS

200g basmati rice
½ tablespoon sesame oil
3 shallots, chopped
1 red chilli, deseeded and chopped
3 garlic cloves, crushed
5cm piece fresh ginger, grated
2 teaspoons curry powder
1 teaspoon ground turmeric
½ small white cabbage, sliced
1 red pepper, deseeded and sliced
150g frozen peas
3 spring onions, trimmed and sliced
2 tomatoes, diced
3 tablespoons soy sauce
1 teaspoon white wine vinegar
4 eggs
Small handful fresh coriander leaves, to garnish

SmartPoints
6 per serving

 See page 6

METHOD

1 Put the basmati rice in a pan with 400ml cold water. Bring to the boil, then reduce to a simmer and cook, covered, for 10-12 minutes, until the water is absorbed. Leave to rest for 5 minutes before fluffing up the grains with a fork.

2 Heat the sesame oil in a large wok over a medium-high heat and add the shallots. Fry for 1-2 minutes, then add the chilli and garlic and continue to cook until softened. Add the ginger, curry powder and turmeric and stir well. Reduce the heat slightly. Add the cabbage and pepper and cook for 2-3 minutes then stir in the peas, spring onions and tomatoes and continue to cook for 2-3 minutes.

3 Add the cooked rice and soy sauce to the wok and toss together until everything is combined.

4 Meanwhile, poach the eggs by bringing a medium-size pan of water to a gentle simmer. Add the vinegar, then gently crack the eggs into different sides of the pan, one at a time. Poach the eggs for 2 minutes until the whites are set, then remove from the water and drain on kitchen paper.

5 Serve the rice topped with a poached egg and garnished with the coriander leaves.

Veggie

TURKISH-STYLE STUFFED AUBERGINES

Roasting the stuffed aubergines really intensifies the flavours – the cheese adds a delicious salty touch.

SERVES 4

PREP TIME 20 minutes + cooling **COOK TIME** 1 hour

INGREDIENTS
4 aubergines, halved lengthways
1 tablespoon olive oil
1 onion, finely chopped
1 celery stick, finely chopped
2 garlic cloves, finely sliced
1 each green, red and yellow pepper, deseeded and sliced into thin strips
1 teaspoon ground cumin
1 teaspoon smoked paprika
½ teaspoon ground cinnamon
2 x 400g tins chopped tomatoes
1 tablespoon red wine vinegar
1 tablespoon pomegranate molasses
120g Weight Watchers Greek Style Salad Cheese, chopped
Fresh mint leaves, to garnish

 SmartPoints
2 per serving

  See page 6

METHOD

1 Preheat the oven to 200°C, fan 180°C, gas mark 6. Using a knife, score the aubergine flesh in a crisscross pattern. Put on a baking tray, brush with half the oil and bake for 30-35 minutes until tender.

2 Meanwhile, heat the remaining oil in a large frying pan over a medium heat and cook the onion and celery for 5 minutes. Add the garlic and fry for 1-2 minutes, then add the peppers and cook for 5 minutes until they start to soften.

3 Stir in the spices and cook for 1 minute. Add the tomatoes, vinegar and pomegranate molasses. Simmer gently for 20 minutes, until the vegetables are tender.

4 Remove the aubergines from the oven, let cool a little, then scoop out the flesh, leaving enough of a shell so the aubergines don't collapse.

5 Stir the aubergine flesh into the tomato and pepper mixture. Season to taste. Spoon into the aubergine shells and bake for 20-25 minutes.

6 Remove from the oven and set aside to cool to room temperature. Serve topped with the cheese and garnished with the mint.

JACKET SWEET POTATO WITH SPICY BAKED BEANS

Home-made baked beans and a dollop of yogurt make the perfect topping for a jacket sweet potato.

SERVES 4

PREP TIME 15 minutes **COOK TIME** 1 hour

INGREDIENTS

4 x 250g sweet potatoes
Calorie controlled cooking spray
1 onion, finely chopped
1 green chilli, finely diced
5cm piece fresh ginger, grated
2 garlic cloves, finely chopped
1 teaspoon ground coriander
1 teaspoon ground cumin
1 teaspoon ground turmeric
3 tablespoons tomato purée
2 x 400g tins cannellini beans, drained and rinsed
1 cinnamon stick
4 tablespoons 0% fat natural Greek yogurt
Handful fresh coriander, leaves picked and chopped

METHOD

1 Preheat the oven to 200°C, fan 180°C, gas mark 6. Mist the sweet potatoes with cooking spray and season. Put the potatoes in a roasting tin and roast for 1 hour or until tender.

2 Halfway through the potato roasting time, mist a large nonstick frying pan with cooking spray and put over a medium-low heat. Add the onion and cook for 6-8 minutes, until softened, adding a splash of water if the pan becomes dry or the onion starts to stick. Add the chilli, ginger and garlic to the pan, and cook for 1 minute. Stir in the spices and tomato purée and cook for a further minute.

3 Add the cannellini beans and cinnamon stick to the pan along with 400ml water and stir to combine. Bring the mixture to the boil, then reduce the heat and simmer, covered, for 10 minutes until thickened. Remove the cinnamon stick and discard.

4 Cut a cross into each baked sweet potato, then spoon over the spicy baked beans. Serve topped with the yogurt and garnished with the coriander.

 SmartPoints
8 per serving

   See page 6

Veggie

ARRABIATA PIZZA WITH MOZZARELLA & OREGANO

Spicy tomato sauce is topped with yellow pepper
and mozzarella to create this deliciously easy pizza.

MAKES 4

PREP TIME 15 minutes **COOK TIME** 40 minutes

INGREDIENTS
Calorie controlled
cooking spray
½ small red onion,
finely chopped
1 garlic clove, crushed
1 red chilli, deseeded and
finely chopped plus extra
slices to serve
200g passata
1 tablespoon dried oregano,
plus extra to scatter
4 Weight Watchers wraps
125g ball light mozzarella,
thinly sliced
1 small yellow pepper,
thinly sliced
1 green chilli, sliced, to serve
60g fresh rocket, to serve

METHOD

1 Preheat the oven to 200°C, fan 180°C, gas mark 6 and put 2 large
baking sheets in the oven to heat up.

2 Mist a heavy-bottomed pan with cooking spray and cook the onion
over a medium heat for 6-8 minutes until soft. Add the garlic and
chilli and cook for another minute. Add the passata and half the
oregano, then simmer over a medium-low heat for 15 minutes
until thickened. Season to taste.

3 Put the wraps onto the hot baking sheets, then spread them with
the sauce, leaving a 2cm border. Top with the mozzarella and
pepper and remaining oregano, then bake for 15 minutes until
crisp and the mozzarella has melted.

4 Top each pizza with the red and green chilli slices and the rocket,
then serve.

6 SmartPoints
6 per pizza

Veggie

MIXED-BEAN VEGGIE CHILLI WITH CORIANDER RICE

Our ultimate veggie chilli is simple to prepare and slow cooks over a low heat for maximum flavour.

SERVES 4

PREP TIME 10 minutes **COOK TIME** 30 minutes

INGREDIENTS

Calorie controlled cooking spray
1 red onion, finely chopped
2 garlic cloves, crushed
1½ teaspoons ground cumin
1½ teaspoons ground coriander
1 teaspoon sweet smoked paprika
1 tablespoon sun-dried tomato purée
1 tablespoon chipotle paste
2 x 400g tins chopped tomatoes
400g tin mixed beans, drained and rinsed
400g tin butter beans, drained and rinsed
2 x 250g packs microwavable basmati rice
Large handful fresh coriander, finely chopped
Finely grated zest and juice of ½ lime, plus extra lime wedges to serve

METHOD

1 Mist a large nonstick pan with cooking spray and cook the onion for 6-8 minutes until soft, then add the garlic, cumin, ground coriander and paprika and cook for a further minute. Stir in the tomato purée and chipotle paste and cook for another minute, then add the tomatoes and simmer over a low heat for 10 minutes. Add the beans and simmer for 5 minutes.

2 Meanwhile, cook the rice to pack instructions, then stir through the fresh coriander and lime zest and juice.

3 Serve the rice and chilli with the lime wedges to squeeze over.

SmartPoints
6 per serving

  See page 6

Veggie

QUORN KORMA WITH CORIANDER CAULIFLOWER 'RICE'

Serving this delicious vegetarian curry with cauliflower 'rice' helps keep the SmartPoints low.

SERVES 4

PREP TIME 10 minutes **COOK TIME** 20 minutes

INGREDIENTS

1 tablespoon olive oil
1 onion, finely chopped
2 garlic cloves, crushed
3cm piece fresh ginger, grated
2 teaspoons tomato purée
1 teaspoon ground cumin
1 teaspoon ground coriander
1 teaspoon ground turmeric
½ teaspoon ground fenugreek
¼ teaspoon chilli powder
275ml vegetable stock, made
with ½ stock cube
700g Quorn
chicken-style pieces
50g sultanas
150g 0% fat natural
Greek yogurt
20 whole almonds, chopped
Calorie controlled
cooking spray
1 whole cauliflower, leaves and
core removed, blitzed in a food
processor to resemble 'rice'
Large handful fresh coriander,
leaves, roughly chopped

METHOD

1 Heat the oil in a large, deep nonstick frying pan over a medium heat. Add the onion and cook for 6-8 minutes, until soft. Add the garlic and ginger and continue to cook for 1 minute. Stir in the tomato purée and spices and cook for 2-3 minutes.

2 Pour in the stock and bring the mixture to the boil. Let bubble for 2-3 minutes, until the sauce starts to reduce.

3 Add the Quorn and sultanas to the pan, and stir to coat. Simmer for 5-6 minutes, until you have a sticky sauce. Stir in the yogurt and cook for 2 minutes, until warmed through. Season to taste then stir in most of the almonds.

4 Meanwhile, mist another large nonstick frying pan with cooking spray and cook the cauliflower 'rice' over a medium heat for 5 minutes until tender. Stir through the coriander, then season to taste.

5 Divide the cauliflower 'rice' and curry between bowls, and serve garnished with the remaining almonds.

SmartPoints
4 per serving

   See page 6

Tip
If you don't have a food processor, you can use the coarse side of a grater to make the cauliflower 'rice'.

Veggie

CARROT & FETA FRITTERS WITH HARISSA DIPPING SAUCE

Perfect for a light lunch, these vegetable fritters are served with a spicy yogurt sauce.

SERVES 4

PREP TIME 15 minutes **COOK TIME** 45 minutes

INGREDIENTS

600g carrots, coarsely grated
5 spring onions, trimmed and finely chopped
1 garlic clove, finely chopped
Large handful fresh coriander, roughly chopped
100g reduced-fat feta, crumbled
4 eggs
2 tablespoons plain flour
Calorie controlled cooking spray
170g 0% fat natural Greek yogurt
1 tablespoon harissa paste
Salad leaves, to serve

SmartPoints
3 per serving

METHOD

1 Wrap the grated carrot in a clean, dry tea towel and squeeze out the excess liquid. Put the carrots in a large bowl with the spring onions, garlic, coriander and feta, and mix to combine.

2 In a separate bowl, whisk together the eggs and flour until you have a smooth mixture. Season then pour over the carrot mixture and stir to combine.

3 Heat a large nonstick frying pan over a medium heat and mist with cooking spray. Working in batches, add heaped spoonfuls of the mixture to the pan, pressing down slightly with the back of the spoon. Cook for 6-8 minutes on each side until golden, then remove from the pan and keep warm. Repeat until you have 12 fritters.

4 To make the sauce, combine the yogurt and harissa paste in a small bowl. Serve the fritters with the salad leaves and the dipping sauce on the side.

TOFU & MUSHROOM STIR-FRY WITH SESAME NOODLES

Sitr-fries are great for getting maximum flavour in a flash. This one teams tasty mushrooms with tofu.

SERVES 4

PREP TIME 15 minutes **COOK TIME** 15 minutes

INGREDIENTS
396g block tofu
180g medium dried egg noodles
½ tablespoon sesame seeds
Calorie controlled cooking spray
200g shiitake or chestnut mushrooms, larger ones halved
100g spring onions, 1 finely sliced, the rest cut into 3cm pieces
2 garlic cloves, crushed
4cm piece fresh ginger, grated
½ stick lemongrass, outer layers removed and the stem very finely chopped
2 small green chillies, deseeded, 1 finely chopped, 1 sliced
Finely grated zest of ½ lime, plus lime wedges to serve
2 sachets Weight Watchers Soy, Chilli & Ginger Dressing

METHOD

1 Drain the tofu, wrap it in kitchen paper and put it on a plate. Top with another plate and settle a few full food tins on top. Leave for 10 minutes, then remove the paper towel and cut the tofu into 3cm cubes.

2 Cook the noodles to pack instructions, drain well then toss with the sesame seeds and set aside.

3 Mist a large nonstick wok with cooking spray, set over a high heat and fry the tofu for 3-4 minutes, until brown on all sides, then transfer to a plate.

4 Mist the wok with more cooking spray, then fry the mushrooms and spring onion pieces for 3-4 minutes. Add the garlic, ginger, lemongrass and chopped chilli and cook for another minute. Add the lime zest and soy, chilli and ginger dressing and toss together, then stir through the noodles.

5 Serve the noodles topped with the tofu, the sliced spring onion and sliced chilli, with the lime wedges on the side.

SmartPoints
5 per serving

Veggie

CHIPOTLE, LIME & BLACK BEAN TACOS WITH SWEETCORN RELISH

Chilli and lime is a great flavour combination that works really well in these veggie tacos.

SERVES 4

PREP TIME 15 minutes **COOK TIME** 25 minutes

INGREDIENTS

Calorie controlled cooking spray
1 onion, finely chopped
2 garlic cloves, crushed
1½ teaspoons mustard powder
198g tin sweetcorn, drained and rinsed
2 tablespoons cider vinegar
1½ teaspoons agave syrup
240g tin black beans, rinsed and drained
2 tablespoons chipotle chilli paste
Finely grated zest and juice of 1 lime, plus lime wedges to serve
4 Weight Watchers Wraps
50g red cabbage, finely shredded
Small handful fresh coriander leaves
1 small red chilli, deseeded and finely sliced

METHOD

1 To make the sweetcorn relish, mist a frying pan with cooking spray and cook the onion over a medium heat for 6-8 minutes until soft. Transfer half of the onion to a bowl and set aside.

2 Add half of the garlic and all of the mustard powder to the pan, and cook for another minute. Stir in the sweetcorn, vinegar and agave syrup. Turn the heat up to high and cook for 2-3 minutes until the liquid has evaporated. Remove from the pan and set aside.

3 Wipe the pan clean, mist with more cooking spray and add the reserved onion and the remaining garlic. Cook for 1 minute, then add the beans and chilli paste. Cook for 2-3 minutes until warmed through, then roughly mash the beans, leaving about a quarter of them whole. Stir in the lime zest and juice, season to taste and remove from the heat. Add a splash of water to the beans mixture, if it's too thick.

4 Toast the wraps in a dry frying pan on both sides until they're just starting to blister, then cut each one in half. Top each half with some of the bean mixture and a handful of cabbage, then spoon over some of the sweetcorn relish. Scatter over the coriander and sliced chilli, then serve with the lime wedges to squeeze over.

SmartPoints
5 per serving

Veggie

LEMONGRASS & GINGER TOFU FRITTERS

Think tofu is lacking in flavour? Try this easy
Thai-style recipe that will change your mind.

SERVES 4

PREP TIME 10 minutes **COOK TIME** 10 minutes

INGREDIENTS
280g firm tofu
3 garlic cloves, finely chopped
1 red chilli, deseeded and
finely chopped
2 lemongrass stalks, outer
leaves removed and stalks
finely chopped
2.5cm piece fresh root
ginger, grated
3 spring onions, trimmed
and finely chopped
3 tablespoons chopped
fresh coriander
1 tablespoon light soy sauce
1 egg white
3 tablespoons plain flour
Calorie controlled
cooking spray
2 limes, halved, to serve

FOR THE CHILLI DIPPING SAUCE
2 tablespoons reduced-fat
mayonnaise
2 tablespoons sweet
chilli sauce
Juice of 1 lime

METHOD

1 Pat the tofu dry with kitchen towel, then coarsely grate it. Squeeze
it in your hands to remove all excess water (this is important to
ensure the mixture holds together well).

2 Put the tofu in a mixing bowl with the garlic, chilli, lemongrass,
ginger, spring onions, coriander, soy sauce, egg white and flour.
Season to taste and stir until combined, then form the mixture into
eight even-size patties.

3 Meanwhile, mix together all the ingredients for the chilli dipping
sauce in a bowl and set aside.

4 Mist a large nonstick frying pan with cooking spray and put over
a medium heat. Cook the fritters, four at a time, for 4-5 minutes
on each side or until golden. Serve two fritters per person with the
dipping sauce and lime halves.

SmartPoints
3 per serving

HARIRA WITH TORTILLA DIPPERS

This vegetarian version of the popular North African soup served with tortillas makes a hearty meal in itself.

SERVES 4

PREP TIME 20 minutes **COOK TIME** 40 minutes

INGREDIENTS

1 tablespoon olive oil
1 onion, finely chopped
1 carrot, peeled and finely chopped
2 celery sticks, finely chopped
2 garlic cloves, crushed
4 teaspoons ras el hanout
500g passata
500ml hot vegetable stock, made using 1 stock cube
3 Weight Watchers Wraps, each one cut into 6 strips
Calorie controlled cooking spray
400g tin chickpeas, drained and rinsed
400g tin green lentils, drained and rinsed
1 tablespoon fresh coriander, chopped
Juice of ½ lemon, plus lemon wedges to serve

METHOD

1 Heat the oil in a medium pan and cook the onion, carrot and celery for 8-10 minutes until they start to soften, then add the garlic and 3 teaspoons of the ras el hanout for another minute, stirring all the time. Add the passata and stock and simmer for 30 minutes.

2 Meanwhile, preheat the oven to 200°C, fan 180°C, gas mark 6. Put the sliced wraps onto a baking sheet, mist with cooking spray and scatter over the remaining ras el hanout, then bake for 10-12 minutes until crisp.

3 Stir the chickpeas and lentils into the soup and simmer for 5 minutes until warmed through, then stir in the coriander and lemon juice. Serve with the wraps on the side and lemon wedges.

SmartPoints
5 per serving

Tip
Ras el hanout is a fragrant spice mix from North Africa. You can also use it as a rub for meat before grilling or roasting it.

Veggie

PIRI PIRI HALLOUMI & SWEET POTATO TRAY BAKE

Halloumi cheese coated in piri piri spices makes this easy vegetable bake extra special.

SERVES 4

PREP TIME 10 minutes **COOK TIME** 45 minutes

INGREDIENTS

450g sweet potato, peeled and cut into 3cm chunks
Calorie controlled cooking spray
200g light halloumi, cut into 8 slices
1 sachet Weight Watchers Spicy Piri Piri Sauce
2 red onions, thickly sliced
180g cherry tomatoes, halved
400g tin chickpeas, drained, rinsed and patted dry
Baby leaf salad, to serve

  SmartPoints
8 per serving

METHOD

1 Preheat the oven to 200°C, fan 180°C, gas mark 6. Put the sweet potato onto a baking tray and mist with cooking spray. Season to taste and roast for 20 minutes until tender.

2 Put the halloumi into a bowl, add the piri piri sauce and toss gently to coat, then add to the tray along with the onions, tomatoes and chickpeas. Mist with cooking spray and return to the oven to cook for another 25 minutes until the halloumi is starting to blister and the sweet potato is tender. Serve with the salad on the side.

Recipe index

MANGE TOUT
Thai yellow fish curry   32
MANGO
Chicken & mango curry GF   54
Jerk chicken traybake with mango salsa   58
Miso roast chicken GF   42
Mixed-bean veggie chilli with coriander rice V GF   96
Moroccan fish tagine with lemon couscous   14
MUSHROOMS
Asian spiced broth with pork balls & cabbage   82
Chicken & chipotle stew with quinoa GF   40
Tofu & mushroom stir-fry with sesame noodles V   102
MUSSELS
Thai-spiced mussels in coconut chilli broth   22

NOODLES
Thai pork curry with coconut noodles   70
Tofu & mushroom stir-fry with sesame noodles V   102

PAK CHOI
Salmon fillets with a ginger & lemongrass crust   28
Thai pork curry with coconut noodles   70
Paprika beef & butter bean goulash GF   62
Paprika fish & fennel stew   30
PASTA
Prawn, chilli & tomato linguine   20
PEAS
Harissa chicken skewers with bulgur wheat salad   38
Miso roast chicken GF   42
Salmon fillets with a ginger & lemongrass crust   28
Spiced nasi goreng V GF   88
Piri piri halloumi & sweet potato traybake V   110
Piri piri pork with roasted pepper rice GF   84
PIZZA
Arrabiata pizza with mozzarella & oregano V   94
PORK
Harissa pork with cumin-spiced 'noodles' GF   64
Piri piri pork with roasted pepper rice GF   84
Sticky Bourbon pork   80
Thai pork curry with coconut noodles   70
PRAWNS
Chilli prawns & chorizo rice bowl GF   26
Paprika fish & fennel stew   30
Prawn, chilli & tomato linguine   20

QUINOA
Chicken & chipotle stew with quinoa GF   40
Quick lamb biryani GF   74
Quorn korma with coriander cauliflower 'rice' V GF   98

RICE
Chicken & mango curry GF   54
Chicken jalfrezi with rice GF   50
Mixed-bean veggie chilli with coriander rice V GF   96
Piri piri pork with roasted pepper rice GF   84
Quick lamb biryani GF   74
Salmon fillets with a ginger & lemongrass crust   28
Spiced nasi goreng V GF   88
Spicy Szechuan turkey mince with green beans GF   48
Thai yellow fish curry   32
Za'atar chicken drumsticks with tahini yogurt GF   56

SALAD
Lamb tikka kebabs with lentils & spicy coleslaw GF   66
Sticky Bourbon pork   80
Za'atar chicken drumsticks with tahini yogurt GF   56
SALMON
Salmon fillets with a ginger & lemongrass crust   28
Salmon Teriyaki burger with wasabi mayonnaise   18
Sausage shakshuka with feta   68
SMOKED SALMON
Cumin-spiced scrambled eggs with smoked salmon   16
Smoky black bean & chorizo soup GF   72
SOUP
Asian spiced broth with pork balls & cabbage   82
Harira with tortilla dippers V   108
Smoky black bean & chorizo soup GF   72
Spiced beef nachos   76
Spiced nasi goreng V GF   88
Spicy Szechuan turkey mince with green beans GF   48
SPINACH
Quick lamb biryani GF   74
Sticky Bourbon pork   80
Sumac baked fish in a bag   24
Sumac chicken kebabs with herby couscous   52
SWEET POTATO
Harissa pork with cumin-spiced 'noodles' GF   64
Jackel sweet potato with spicy baked beans V GF   92
Jerk chicken traybake with mango salsa   58
Piri piri halloumi & sweet potato tray bake V   110

TACOS
Chipotle, lime & black bean tacos
   with sweetcorn relish V   104
Thai pork curry with coconut noodles   70
Thai-spiced mussels in coconut chilli broth   22
Thai yellow fish curry   32
TOFU
Lemongrass & ginger tofu fritters V   106
Tofu & mushroom stir-fry with sesame noodles V   102
TORTILLAS
Spiced beef nachos   76
TURKEY
Spicy Szechuan turkey mince with green beans GF   48
Turkish-style stuffed aubergines V GF   90

Za'atar chicken drumsticks with tahini yogurt GF   56

113

SmartPoints index

SmartPoints™